IT'S TRUE!

YOU EAT

POISON

EVERY DAY

IT'S TRUE!

Did you know that frogs are cannibals,
fashion can be fatal and the dinosaurs
never died? Or that redheads were
once burned at the stake as witches?
Find out why rubbish tips are like lasagna,
and how maggots help solve crimes!

Books to make
your brain bulge!
find out all about them on
www.itstrue.com.au

Peter Macinnis

PICTURES BY **Bettina Guthridge**

IT'S TRUE! YOU EAT POISON EVERY DAY

ALLEN&UNWIN

First published in 2006

Allen & Unwin
83 Alexander Street
Crows Nest NSW 2065
Australia
Phone: (61 2) 8425 0100
Fax: (61 2) 9906 2218
Email: info@allenandunwin.com
Web: www.allenandunwin.com

National Library of Australia
Cataloguing-in-Publication entry:

Macinnis, Peter.
It's true! you eat poison every day.
Bibliography.
Includes index.
For children.
ISBN 1 74114 626 7.
1. Poisons – Juvenile literature. I. Guthridge, Bettina.
II. Title. (Series: It's true; 18)
615.9

Series, cover and text design by Ruth Grüner
Cover photographs: RubberBall Productions/Getty Images
Set in 12.5pt Minion by Ruth Grüner
Printed by McPherson's Printing Group

1 3 5 7 9 10 8 6 4 2

**Teaching notes for the It's True! series are available
on the website: www.itstrue.com.au**

CONTENTS

WHY POISONS?

My dentist said, 'I've just given you a lethal injection.'

He explained that the novocaine he'd just injected into my jaw was fatal – or would be if it went into a vein. Where it was, in the muscle, the injection was safe.

In researching this book, I discovered that poisons are used as beauty aids and medicines as well as for murder and war. I read stories of kings and queens who thought each meal might be their last. (Elizabeth I had guards to taste-test her food in case it was poisoned and people to check inside her gloves.) I read about criminals who botched the job, and explorers who ate their dogs. I found out why green dresses were once so dangerous and why we should beware of Botox. It's true, poisons are everywhere. The good news is that you won't die of them – at least probably not today . . .

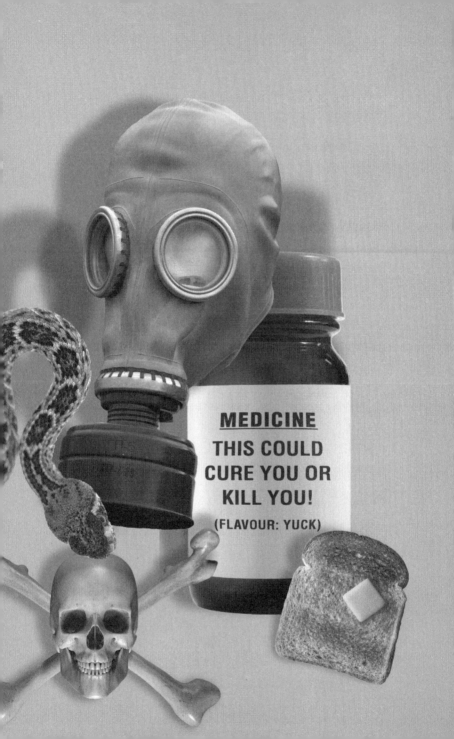

1

'KNOCK 'EM OUT WITH A MICKEY FINN': POISONS AND FOOD

Is everyone who uses poison a criminal? If they were, then your mum and dad and grandparents would be in jail – and so would you. You probably use something toxic every day. Detergent under the sink, turps in the garage, snailkiller in the shed, nail-polish remover, lubricant, glues,

This is a
TOXIC
substance

nappy cleaner . . . they're all labelled 'Poison'. Your local supermarket is full of these ordinary poisons, no-good-for-murder poisons, and they have many uses. (Why are they no good for murder? You'll find out in chapter 8.)

That's not all. There are poisons in the fruitbowl and the pantry. You could die of coffee poisoning, salt poisoning or potato poisoning. Why don't you? Because you don't eat or drink enough of them. We know that 100 cups of coffee, 250 grams (9 ounces) of salt or 200 kilograms (440 pounds) of potatoes will kill an adult if taken all at once.

There's cyanide in apple pips – not a lot, but enough to give pips a bitter taste. Enough to kill a really determined apple-pip chomper. Even the oxygen we need to breathe can be lethal – pure oxygen, that is. If you breathe pure oxygen, your

WARNING COFFEE KILLS!

Vitamins, anyone?

Australian explorer Douglas Mawson led an expedition to the Antarctic. He and two companions, Belgrave Ninnis and Xavier Mertz, were struggling back to base camp when Ninnis fell into a deep crevasse. With him went the sledge containing most of the food. Mawson and Mertz soon had nothing left to eat but their husky dogs. The meat was stringy, so they ate the soft livers, which were easier to chew.

They became very ill – dizzy, nauseous and irritable. Strips of their skin and hair peeled away, and so did the soles of Mawson's feet. Mertz died before they got back to base, and Mawson nearly did.

We now know that the dogs' livers contained large amounts of Vitamin A – far too much for a human to eat safely. Mawson learned the hard way that we all need a small amount of Vitamin A, but too much will kill us.

lungs fill with fluid and break down. Premature babies used to go blind when they were kept in 100 per cent oxygen.

DUNCAN GOW'S SANDWICH

Gow was a poor (and unlucky) Edinburgh tailor whose children brought him a parsley sandwich. The 'parsley' was really hemlock, which they'd picked by mistake.[1] During the next three hours, the tailor was gradually paralysed, but he stayed conscious and clear-headed till just before he died.

[1] Ordinary hemlock looks just like parsley. There is another kind, water hemlock, which looks a bit like a turnip. It causes convulsions and dreadful pains.

In 1867, a doctor called Harley dosed himself with small amounts of hemlock. He then said it would be a good treatment for hyperactive children – in low doses, of course! The suggestion was never taken up. I wonder why?

KILLING OFF SOCRATES

The story of Socrates shows that the ancient Greeks knew all about hemlock. Socrates was a philosopher and he asked questions that showed up people who were silly or dishonest. When things were wrong, he said so. That really annoyed the people who were in power in Athens. They charged him with 'corrupting the young', found him guilty, and voted for him to be executed. In those days, that was done by giving the condemned person a dose of hemlock, and then sitting around waiting for him to die. Plato, another philosopher who had been a student of Socrates', described it.

The man . . . kept his hand upon Socrates, and after a while examined his feet and legs; then pinched his foot hard and asked him if he felt it. Socrates said no. Then he did the same to his legs; and moving gradually up in this way let us see that he was getting cold and numb. Presently he felt him again and said that when it reached the heart, Socrates would be gone.

The Athenians thought they were getting rid of a problem by killing Socrates, but they also succeeded in making him more famous. People have remembered him down to this day. Otherwise, he might have been just another philosopher, like, umm, what's-his-name.

DEADLY COLOURS

Foods sell better if they look good. In the
past, wicked people would add anything to
food if it meant they could charge more
for it. Shopkeepers and manufacturers
began colouring the foods they sold.
Margarine (which is naturally
white) could
be stained
to a nice
butter-yellow
with toxic
aniline dyes,
until dairy
farmers

managed to get laws making it illegal in most places.
In Britain, Bath buns were coloured yellow with
lead chromate, or even with arsenic sulfide. This was
definitely not good for the customer. Bakers found the
poisons very profitable, though, because bun-buyers
liked the nice colour.

Sometimes dye even replaced the food. The makers of one type of cider claimed it was prepared from concentrated apple juice. Scientists found the 'cider' was made of sugar, fruit essence and aniline dye, with not even a trace of apple juice.

There were even nastier tricks. Used tea-leaves would be shaken up with soapstone (a sort of clay) and a paint pigment called Prussian blue to make them look new. Poor-quality new tea-leaves might have iron sulfate added to make the leaves look nicer. This was back in the 1800s. Now we have laws and labels that help prevent such tricks.

Probably nobody was killed by these additives, but preservatives are much more dangerous.

PRESERVATIVES

Food can be made to last longer by treating it with chemicals that are poisonous to germs and moulds. Rather than call these 'poisons' (which might put customers off), manufacturers call them 'preservatives'. Some preservatives, like the sugar in jam and the

salt in corned beef, are not dangerous to us, even though they kill germs. Others are highly poisonous – for example, formalin was added to meat and milk foods. It was also used to embalm the dead! Formalin is still used to preserve noodles and tofu in some parts of the world.

The ancient Romans often added poisonous lead acetate to wine to stop it changing to vinegar. We call the substance 'sugar of lead', because it tastes sweet. The Romans thought the sweetness improved their wine.

 **We know that people were using lead as a preservative and sweetener for beef In the 1600s. During the Great Fire of London (1666), the lead coffin of a man called John Colet was exposed to view. Two scientists made a hole in the coffin and found it was full of sweet-tasting liquid. Their friend John Aubrey said, 'Perhaps it was a Pickle, as for Beefe'.**

POISON AT THE PUB

There are many legends of fearful mixtures put together in Australian bush shanties and served to the men who tramped the bush looking for work as shearers and farmhands. Almost anything that made people woozy was suspected of going into 'the grog'. But it didn't start in the outback. Dubious mixtures had been sold in Britain long before.

Levant nut was a poisonous berry that the English imported from India. They used it to make poisoned wheat that could be spread around to kill pests. It wasn't only farmers that found it useful. Some English hotel-owners were mixing beer with water and salt to cut costs. Then they added levant nut, which made people feel confused. This stopped the customers realising that there was less alcohol in the watered-down beer. In the end, the hotel-keepers were caught out when local doctors noticed that people using the inn showed similar signs of illness, including fits. Luckily, nobody died.

FETCH ME SAILORS, BY HOOK OR BY CROOK

Centuries ago, sailors knew that going to sea was risky. They would avoid long hauls, trips that might take a year or more before they got home again. Ship-owners found it hard to raise a crew. Ships' captains used to pay innkeepers to knock men out with a 'Mickey Finn' – poison drops added to a drink. The trick was to get the dose right, so as to knock them out, not kill them. One common drug was chloral hydrate, used by doctors to make patients sleep. Other more dangerous poisons could also have been used, but the people using them preferred not to say too much.

Once the victims were unconscious, they could be carried off to a ship that was waiting to leave. By the time they came around, they were out at sea and there was no escape. They would often 'jump ship' at the next port, though. Quite a few American families began with somebody who had been kidnapped and then had jumped ship to escape.

2

'HOW SOFT YOUR SKIN IS, MY DEAR':

POISONS AND BEAUTY

Would you risk poisoning yourself, just for the sake of your appearance? Some people would – they'd do just about anything to make themselves look better.

HAIRLESS AND CARELESS

After the metal thallium was discovered in 1861, scientists found that it made people's hair fall out. Later they discovered it was poisonous. Thallium was sold as rat poison. It was also given to children by doctors (in small doses) to rid them of headlice. If the dose was right, the children completely lost their hair on the 16th to 18th day. These days, we treat headlice with poisons that don't need to be swallowed.

In France, thallium was used by people who had ringworm, an itchy skin fungus that often grows on the scalp. Once the hair was out of the way, suitable chemicals (poisons, of course!) could be used to kill the fungus.

There is a story that the CIA wanted to use a thallium poison on Fidel Castro, the leader of Cuba, to make his beard fall out. They thought this would embarrass Castro. If this is true, it's one of the silliest poison plots ever!

DYING TO BE DARK

Some people hate the idea of getting old, and use dyes to hide grey and white hairs. In the past, the dyes often contained lead, which reacted with sulfur in the hair to make black lead sulfide. Other hair dyes contained silver, and they were less poisonous, but could leave people with burns on their scalp, or a grey colour in their skin. These days, dyes are tested and so they are fairly safe.

FATAL FACIALS?

In the time of Queen Elizabeth I (the late 1500s), people thought that women with pale faces were the most beautiful. Elizabeth and her court ladies began painting their faces with white lead. Good Queen Bess was always on the alert for poisoners – she should have checked her make-up!

In later centuries, women used to put arsenic oxide on their face to make their skin pale and also smooth. There was just one problem. Once you'd started using arsenic, you couldn't stop. If you did, your skin aged very quickly, and looked worse than if you had never put on anything at all. Arsenic is a cumulative poison – the more you build up or accumulate in your body, the sicker you'll get – so using arsenic on your skin was a bit like taking a ride on a tiger. But for some women, looking good counted for more than surviving.

The sad story of Elizabeth Siddal . . .

Elizabeth Siddal was an artist's model who married a painter and poet called Dante Gabriel Rossetti. She was a great arsenic user, because she wanted to retain her youthful looks, bright eyes and clear complexion. Apparently she knew that once she'd started she wouldn't be able to stop, but she went ahead anyway. In the end she suicided, by taking an overdose of a medicine called laudanum.

. . . whose husband dug up her coffin

Seven years after her death, in 1869, Rossetti asked for permission to have his wife dug up from her grave in a London cemetery. He had put in her coffin the only copies of some of his poems, and now he wanted his verses back. The evil-smelling book was disinfected, then dried and copied. The poems were published in 1870, to great literary excitement.

GREEN AND GHASTLY GOWNS

When chemists discovered that some chemicals containing copper and arsenic made beautiful green colours, they were delighted. It took longer for them to discover that the new dyes were highly poisonous.

The copper–arsenic dyes were used mostly in wallpaper and in silk fabric for grand ladies to wear. These dyes were very popular because they didn't fade.

In the 1800s, grand ladies wore many layers of clothing, and so they used to sweat a lot, especially when dancing. (Polite people called it perspiration.) If they had stockings or a gown that was dyed with copper and arsenic, they would absorb some of it through their skin, and get sick, or even die.

Wallpaper dyed this beautiful green was even more dangerous. The first thing people noticed was that bedbugs died in rooms papered with green wallpaper. 'Good!' they thought.

But when they noticed that larger animals like people also died in these rooms, it seemed less good. So what happened?

In those days, rooms were heated with fires, windows were closed, and building walls usually let damp through more than buildings do today. The rooms would get clammy, making the glue under the wallpaper soggy. The glue was made from boiled-down meat or fish – perfect food for fungi.

Slowly, wallpaper dye would seep into the soggy glue. The fungi turned the poisons into a gas called Gosio gas or diethylarsine (the name tells us the gas contains arsenic). The trouble was that the gas got out to where people were. Quite a few mysterious deaths in the nineteenth century were probably caused by arsenic escaping from the wallpaper.

 The famous last words of Oscar Wilde, just before he died.

Either that wallpaper goes, or I do !!

The mystery of the dead emperor

It seems that the Emperor Napoleon of France may have been poisoned with arsenic. The doctors who examined his body thought that he died of cancer, but recent tests on samples of his hair showed fairly high levels of arsenic.

Was the arsenic put in Napoleon's food by someone who wanted to poison him? Did he take arsenic to develop immunity (see chapter 3)? Or did it come from his wallpaper. We don't know. Napoleon was kept in a damp stone house on St Helena, an island in the South Atlantic Ocean, and it seems likely that it had green wallpaper made with copper–arsenic dyes.

arsenic

strand of hair

BOTOX

When journalists look for a good story about terrorists using poison, they talk about botulinum toxin, or the illness it causes, botulism. We also know it as Botox, the stuff people use to get rid of wrinkles on their faces!

Botox was used first to treat 'lazy eye' and uncontrolled blinking. The idea was to use tiny doses, just enough to paralyse the muscle for a few months. As it was being 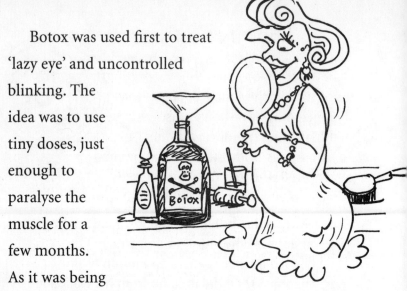 tested, researchers noticed that their patients' faces were smoothing out. Botox really is a deadly poison, but it does take away the lines that people get at the corners of their eyes and on their foreheads as they grow older. It does this by paralysing the muscles that tighten up and make the face look wrinkled.

Some people have had minor allergic reactions, or a bit of bruising from the injection, but nobody has died of the tiny dose used. It is good for the looks of the customers and even better for the people who sell it, because after six to 12 months the wrinkles come back and the customers need a new set of injections!

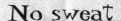

No sweat

Botox also has some rather more important effects for people who sweat badly. Called hyperhidrosis, the sweating causes embarrassment because these people get really wet even when they use pads and anti-perspirants. The quick fix is a Botox injection into the underarm skin, the palms of the hands or the soles of the feet. It paralyses the sweat glands for six to 12 months.

DON'T KOHL ME, I'LL KOHL YOU

When you see movies about ancient Egyptians, the actors always have black make-up around their eyes. The real ancient Egyptians also did, at least when they dressed up – we know this from wall paintings in tombs. They used kohl, or antimony sulphide mixed with soot. Antimony is a poison, and soot often contains poisons that cause cancer, so kohl was a double danger.

Italian ladies used to put belladonna in their eyes to make them look brighter and more attractive. Belladonna made the black central part of the eye, the pupil, look larger. 'Belladonna' means 'beautiful lady' in Italian, but the plant it was made from had a more sinister name. It is called deadly nightshade. If you swallow enough of the juice of the leaf or the berries, your heart will beat faster, the pupils of your eyes will enlarge, you'll feel as though you're suffocating, you'll have hallucinations, and then you'll collapse.

Funnily enough, this poison is also an antidote! Belladonna is used to treat poisoning from opium, chloroform and some nerve poisons.

3

'BUY ME AN ANTIDOTE':

PROFITS FROM POISONS

In ancient times, there were four main ways you could benefit from poisons.

- You could kill somebody to get their money or their job or their throne.
- You could sell poisons to people who wanted to kill others.

- You could have a job as poison-taster for a king or queen who feared poisoning.
- You could sell antidotes to people who feared poisons.

Selling antidotes was the best, because poisoners often get caught and if you sold a poison that didn't work the customers would want their money back. If you sold an antidote that didn't work, there would be no complaints from the customer – they'd be dead!

THE PERILS OF POISON

Selling poison was also a nice little earner, even if it was a bit risky. In Roman times, for example, a woman called Locusta sold the poisons that killed at least six members of the Roman imperial family, perhaps more. She was condemned to death once, and was pardoned by the emperor Nero (who remained one of her customers), but in the end the emperor Galba had her executed, just to be on the safe side.

In 1600, at the court of Queen Elizabeth I of England, a German visitor described how the Yeomen of the Guard entered in scarlet and gold, each carrying a gold plate of food. Then a lady-in-waiting gave each guard a mouthful of the food from the plate he'd carried, just in case he had slipped something nasty into it. (Unlucky if someone *else* had done so.)

The Queen and her advisers had reason to be suspicious. England was at war with Spain, and Mary Queen of Scots was plotting against Elizabeth.

Punishment was severe. A foreign doctor was hanged, drawn and quartered[2] because people thought he was planning to poison the Queen. To protect her, court officials not only tested her food, they also checked her gloves and handkerchiefs for any signs of poison and gave her weekly doses of antidotes. Lots of people at her court had good jobs because the Queen and her advisers feared poison. If you asked them, they would have said poisons were *really* useful for them!

POISONOUS PLANTS IN PONTUS

In ancient times, most poisons came from ordinary herb gardens. Why? Because poison plants like rhubarb, hemlock and deadly nightshade were also

---

[2] What does hanged, drawn and quartered mean? Legend has it that you were hanged for a while, then before you died you were cut down and your entrails (guts)were drawn (or pulled) out, and then you were chopped into four quarters. Some historians disagree. They say that drawing involved being hauled through the streets while people threw things at you. Whichever way it happened, it was no fun for the victim.

used as medicines. These gardens were often managed by old women or servants. That was enough to worry important men.

Mithridates was the king of Pontus, in the part of the world that we now call Turkey. Pontus had many poisonous plants, and 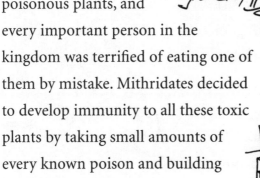 every important person in the kingdom was terrified of eating one of them by mistake. Mithridates decided to develop immunity to all these toxic plants by taking small amounts of every known poison and building the doses up gradually.

Another version of his story says Mithridates collected together all the antidotes he could discover, and mixed them up to make a 'universal antidote', which he then drank. How did he

know it worked? According to the Romans, who loved stories about poison, he tested the poisons and antidotes on prisoners. Then again, the Romans said the same thing about Cleopatra, so maybe it was just a yarn.

Maybe Mithridates was onto a good thing, but then again maybe he wasn't. In 63 BCE, his kingdom of Pontus was invaded by a Roman army. Rather than be disgraced by capture, Mithridates decided to commit suicide. There was just one problem. The quick and easy way out was to take poison, but no matter how much he took, Mithridates could not die. In the end, he had to make his bodyguard stab him to death.

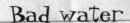

Bad water

Mithridates must have been lucky enough not to take small doses of any of the cumulative poisons. In Bangladesh, Vietnam and many other countries around the world, people are slowly poisoned, every day, by small amounts of arsenic in their water supply. Over time, the arsenic collects in their bodies, building up until they get very sick and eventually die. They do *not* develop immunity to poisons like this.

ANT-HILL ANTIDOTES

If people are frightened of poison, it is easy to persuade them to pay out good money for cures, antidotes, and other sorts of protection. In a time when people had little understanding of how poisons worked, some of the solutions were – well, strange.

One of them was called the bezoar, a small 'stone' found in the stomachs of wild Persian goats, cows, and a few other animals. It was just calcium phosphate, which is found in bones. It would form a 'stone' in the stomach, and be found when the animal was slaughtered. Because they were a bit mysterious, bezoars were sold as antidotes, at great profit to the sellers, who found poison was very good for them indeed.

The best antidotes, according to some of the sellers, were made from jewels. They *would* say that, wouldn't they? The more expensive the supposed ingredients, the more the sellers could charge. (There are three rules in quack medicine. If it tastes bad, people *think* it must be good. If it makes them really sick, they *feel* sure it is good. If it costs a lot, then they are absolutely *certain* it is good.)

A Roman writer called Pliny had an answer to the poisoned bite of a stellion, a kind of spotted lizard. According to Pliny, 'a scorpion stamped' was just the thing. Whether you swallowed it, put the squashed animal on the bite, or just stamped on the scorpion, he did not say. (Whatever you did, it would have saved you from the stellion's poison, because the stellion isn't poisonous.)

Pliny also wrote that if you take the liver of a frog and lay it out near an ant-hill, you will see that the ants only eat one of the two lobes of the liver. According to Pliny, you should then pick it up, dust off the ants, and use that lobe of the liver (and only that lobe) to cure cases of poisoning.

Try out a tryacle

Then there was a doctor called Nicander, who served a king called Attalus, in a place not far from Pontus. Attalus was terrified of poisons. Always willing to earn a fat reward and please his boss, Nicander started a whole tradition of antidotes and medicines that comes right down to the present day.

Nicander wrote a book called *Theriaca* – more of a long poem, actually – about the bites of poisonous animals and how to treat them. From that, we got the name 'theriac' as a general name for antidotes. By about 1600, a theriac or theriacal was a mixture used to prevent disease. The main part of most of these theriacals, or tryacles, as they were called in England, was sugar. You can still buy a tryacle today, but now all the other medicines are missing, and we just call it treacle.

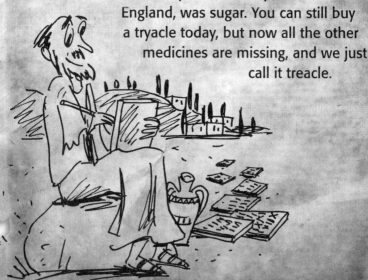

4

'EAR, WHAT'S GOING ON?':
POISONS IN THE WORKPLACE

Sometimes we use poison because it's useful or cheap. In this way, poisons can be good for us, even if they are making us sick at the same time.

POISONED BY PIGMENTS

Painters want their paintings to last. The problem in the past was how to make colours that kept their intensity and didn't fade. Colours made from vegetable dyes did fade. Paints made with metals like mercury, lead, chromium and arsenic made brilliant paintings that glowed on the canvas and lasted forever, or almost. The painters didn't do so well. Many of them were poisoned by their pigments, and went mad or died. Candido Portinari (1903–1962) was a Brazilian artist who liked the strong contrasts that he got from using white lead and colours based on arsenic. He ended up in hospital with arsenic poisoning when he was 45, and later died of lead poisoning.

Even artists working in watercolours and crayon would often use white lead to produce highlights in their work. It seemed that if you wanted to be remembered as a great artist, you had to work with poisons.

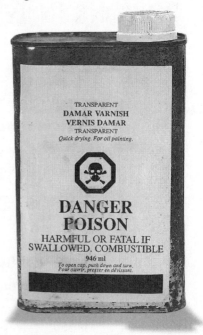

TRANSPARENT
DAMAR VARNISH
VERNIS DAMAR
TRANSPARENT
Quick drying. For oil painting.

DANGER
POISON
HARMFUL OR FATAL IF
SWALLOWED. COMBUSTIBLE
946 ml
To open cap, push down and turn.
Pour ouvrir, presser en dévissant.

VINCENT'S ODD DIET

If you ask people to
name a mad painter,
most of them would say
'Vincent van Gogh', just like
that. After all, Vincent *did*
cut his ear off, and he
used to eat his oil
paints and drink the
turpentine that he
kept to 'thin' the paints.
But did that prove he was mad, or did his strange diet
make him mad?

Dr Gachet, who told us about Vincent's habits,
thought the odd diet was the cause. Then again,
Vincent painted two portraits of his doctor, and
each time there was a stem of foxglove in the picture.
Foxglove is a poisonous plant that was sometimes used
to treat heart disease. Was Gachet treating Vincent for a
heart ailment? We will never know.

LOADS OF LEAD

White lead was used in the 1800s to make paint, glazed pottery and putty. It brought in money for the factory owners, but it was horribly dangerous to the factory workers who made it.

White lead was mainly lead carbonate. It used to be made by the Old Dutch process, where strips of lead metal are buried in bark with vinegar. This would be left alone until the lead had changed to lead carbonate, a white powder.

Writer Robert Sherard described one woman who worked in a lead factory in Newcastle, England. A 'meagre [thin] little woman', she had to carry three trays of white lead at a time out of the chamber where it was made. They weighed 33 kilograms (73 pounds) and she laboured on year after year with this dangerous

Curious about colic

In 1786, two years before Australia was founded, an American scientist called Benjamin Franklin got curious about lead poisoning. In one of his letters, he lists a whole range of people who suffered from 'colic', the name for lead poisoning in those days. We'd call it stomach pains. Most of the victims worked with lead, like plumbers, glaziers (glass-cutters) and painters, but there was a small mystery: some of the patients were stonemasons and soldiers.

Then Franklin was told that stonemasons used lead to fit iron rails into stonework, while soldiers were often hired to grind lead-based pigments for painters. (Soldiers were probably more affected by loading muskets – they did this by spitting a lead ball down the musket barrel.) Either way, Franklin had shown that lead was a dangerous poison. Yet people kept using it – because they could make money from it.

load. Young girls did the same in factories around the country. Why? The answer is simple: they either took the job or they starved. In a sad sort of way, poison kept them alive, until they died. As they worked, they breathed the dust, or it got into their food, where it damaged the nerves and the brain.

POTS, PIPES AND POWER POLES

The glazes that make porcelain and china smooth and shiny used to contain dangerous amounts of lead. (They still may, if the pots are made by back-yard amateurs.) At the start of the twentieth century, pottery was used in all sorts of ways: the insulators on power poles and telephone poles were all porcelain, and so were baths, toilets, basins, dishes and plates. Even sewerage pipes were glazed pottery. All of these items were made with lead-based glazes. Somebody had to make the white lead, then other people had to grind up the lead oxides and apply them to the pots.

Bad for babies

Until about 1980, books were printed using the 'hot metal' process – by inking metal type and pressing it onto the paper. The type was made from lead, tin and antimony. Both lead and antimony are poisonous – bad news for those who worked in printing, or their families.

In 1930s Milan, 150 out of every 1000 children born would die in their first year of life. Worse, 320 out of every 1000 babies of women linked with printing died before they turned one. The printing industry was not good for the babies of Milan.

SOMETHING FISHY HERE

White lead later became a
danger for people living in
old homes. If your house is
more than 60 years old, it's
likely that some of the paint
in it contains white lead.
Sanding off this paint (and
creating lead-laden dust) is
not good for you or your
parents or the family
pets – even goldfish in a
bowl in the next room.

DANGER AT WORK

Poison is still a problem in many workplaces, especially
in poorer countries, where government inspectors can
be paid to 'not notice' dangerous situations. In a case
like that, factory owners can 'cut corners' and save
money, which increases their profits.

In 1984, there was a bad leak at an insecticide factory at Bhopal in India. The insecticide that was made there, carbaryl, is not all that poisonous, but the process used a compound called methyl isocyanate (MIC) that really *was* a nasty poison. Huge amounts of MIC escaped, killing at least 3000 people and maybe 20 000.

Even in Australia, men who work with organic solvents are more likely to have their wives lose babies through a miscarriage. It seems that working with paints, plastics and pesticides can be dangerous.

The other problem with industry is that toxic waste has to go somewhere. Sometimes it is just dumped, and escapes later. Love Canal in America and Lekkerkerk in the Netherlands are famous cases. Homebush Bay, just near the site of the Sydney 2000 Olympics, also carries a load of several different poisons (DDT, heavy metals, dioxins and others) from the chemical factories that used to be there. The dioxins seem to have caused deformities in local fish and are known to be dangerous for humans. They were present in the Agent Orange defoliant that was used in the Vietnam War.

Sus sushi

When Viktor Yushchenko was seeking election as
president of the Ukraine in 2004, he came down
with a mysterious illness that made him feel
unwell, and caused a dreadful skin rash which
looked remarkably like dioxin poisoning. Later tests
showed that he had in fact consumed dioxin.

before

after

His political opponents suggested that he had eaten
'some bad sushi', but Yushchenko, who became
president in early 2005, was definitely poisoned
with dioxin. His opponents later suggested that he
might have poisoned himself to get sympathy.

THE PAIN OF POISON

Plays and operas often have a scene with someone being poisoned. Heroes and heroines, villains and villainesses usually get their dose, say a few words (or sing a lot of words, in opera) and quietly faint. This is wrong.

Poisons work by interfering with the way your body works, and that is just as painful as being shot or stabbed. Most poisons make us vomit, they give us diarrhoea, they give us cramps, they make us drowsy, they give us fits. In just about all cases, poisons will make you feel very sick and very worried. Poison is *not* painless, and it usually leaves a very messy body.

In 1881, a doctor produced a little book, known
to generations of doctors as *Murrell's Poisons*. I own a
14th edition, printed in 1934, so I know what signs of
poisoning a doctor would have looked for, and how a
doctor would have treated it. Here are a few examples:

Arsenic or arsenic oxide is almost tasteless, so it can
be added to food. A fatal dose causes the victim to feel
faint, to vomit and get cramps, about 15 minutes later.
It often takes several painful hours to die. Smaller doses
can cause a very slow poisoning that is just as deadly
in the end.

Belladonna (also called atropine or deadly
nightshade) used to be sold as eye-drops, and it was
injected as a cure for sciatica. Victims feel hot and get
very thirsty, but have trouble swallowing. They become

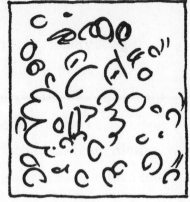

very excited, and then fall into a deep sleep.

Botox causes drooping eyelids and slurred speech. Arms and legs become paralysed, and then the muscles that are used to breathe seize up as well, so that victims suffocate.

Carbon monoxide makes people giddy to start with, then they get a headache and later fall into a coma. When victims' bodies are examined after death, their blood is cherry-red in colour. This is because carbon monoxide locks onto the haemoglobin in our blood, blocking the places where oxygen is normally carried, so the victims die of a lack of oxygen.

Cyanide causes a burning pain in the stomach, the victim foams at the mouth, loses power in the arms and legs, goes into convulsions and dies soon after.

Digitalis makes the victim vomit and have severe diarrhoea. He or she has a headache and gets tired, then delirious, suffers convulsions or fits, and finally goes into a coma and dies.

Kohl today often contains large amounts of lead, and kohl in ancient times was made with antimony, which is much like lead, so using too much kohl as an eyeliner gives symptoms like those of lead poisoning.

Lead compounds are usually slow poisons, gradually building up in the body. Victims have dry throats, severe thirst and stomach pains. With small doses over time, lead will cause brain and nerve damage. With larger doses, the victims' legs become paralysed and they go into convulsions.

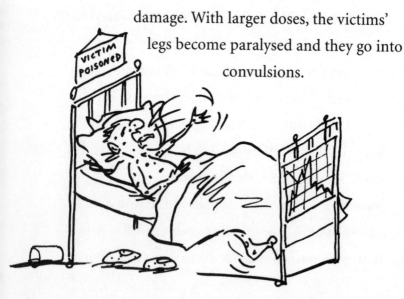

Ricin makes people vomit, feel great pain, and eventually die. It kills cells in the body. The poison comes from castor oil seeds, and as few as three seeds can be fatal.

Snake venoms Most snake venoms interfere with the nerves, which causes paralysis and death. Other snake venoms clot the blood, others cause internal bleeding. Most people who die of snakebite were either trying to catch or kill a snake. To avoid snakebite, leave snakes alone.

Strychnine was once used a lot in preparing baits for pest animals. The poison causes great pain and convulsions. It's produced by several plants[3] as a way of discouraging animals from eating it. Death often comes when the muscles used in breathing are paralysed.

Tetrodotoxin is the most amazing poison of all. Nobody knows what makes it (probably a tiny microbe), but many animals manage to harvest and store it. It causes paralysis, then death. There are myths claiming that this toxin is used in creating zombies.

[3] One of these plants was called *nux vomica* – vomit nut.

5

'GET THE ENEMY':

POISON IN WAR

Is it all right to use poison to fight wars? For a short
while, from 1915 to 1918, people thought it was –
better than any other way of fighting, they said.

HANNIBAL AND THE SNAKES

Hannibal was a famous general in the ancient world.
He was the man who took elephants over the Italian
Alps to fight the Romans. Hannibal's army was
defeated that time, but he escaped and continued
with his campaign. He once won a naval battle against

some allies of Rome by using a sort of poison.

Fighting ships in those days were powered by oarsmen – many men sitting close together and rowing in time with each other. Hannibal sent people out to collect snakes and told them to put the snakes in big pots and jars. Next he told them to throw jars of snakes into the enemy ships. The rowers laughed, until they realised what was coming out of the jars. Panic! They all rowed away as fast as they could, and Hannibal's reputation as a clever fighter was made.

NAPOLEON THE POISONER (OR, LOUIS' NARROW ESCAPE FROM CARROTS)

Remember the emperor Napoleon of France, the one who may have been poisoned with arsenic? It looks as though he tried to poison the French king he had replaced.

In 1804, King Louis XVIII of France was living with his family in exile, in Poland. One of Louis' servants was approached by some strangers and offered a small fortune to add some hollow, poison-filled carrots to the king's soup. The servant was loyal – he accepted the carrots, then told Louis about the plot. Too late: the people who had offered him the money escaped. It turned out that the carrots were filled with a paste of white, yellow and red arsenic.

CARROT

In 1870, Napoleon III of France suggested that French bayonets be tipped with cyanide during the Franco-Prussian War. Perhaps he was just joking, given that cyanide is also known as 'Prussic acid' – anyway, his idea met with horror. These scruples about using poison in battles would not last.

GOING WITH GAS

World War I was a mess. Both sides got bogged down, literally, in muddy trenches in France and Flanders, each side trying to wear the other down. In Turkey, the ANZACs[4] and the Turks got bogged down in much the same way.

Three days before the ANZACs landed at Gallipoli, on 22 April 1915, the German army tried to break through the British defences in Flanders by using chlorine gas.

[4] ANZAC is short for Australian and New Zealand Army Corps.

After that there were many attempts to use poison gases to get a speedy result. The use of gas was all right, some people said, because it made soldiers ill. That meant they could not fight, and had to be cared for. This was better, said these people, than blowing the enemy up with high explosives or making holes in them!

What happened? Troops were told to pee on their socks and breathe through them! Then they were given chemical-soaked gas capes, and given gas masks, and the war went on for another three and a half years. Forty and 50 years later, men were still dying from the damage caused to their lungs during the war.

Peace but not safety

After World War I, the world had far too many battleships, and too many unemployed men. Some of the old soldiers were given the job of cutting up ships that were being scrapped.

There was just one problem: under the grey paint that made the iron ships hard to see, there was a layer of red lead, put there to stop the iron rusting. So some of the soldiers who had avoided lead bullets or poisonous gas in the war ended up poisoned by lead fumes in peacetime.

In World War II (1939–1945), British spies and secret agents were given 'L-pills'. These contained enough cyanide to kill a person in a few seconds. If caught by the enemy, a spy could choose to kill himself or herself by swallowing the L-pill rather than face torture.

6

'PASS THE PILLS, PLEASE': POISONS AS MEDICINES

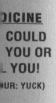

You may have heard about depressed people who have taken their own life by taking an overdose of pills. As the old doctors always said, 'A poison in a small dose is a medicine, and a medicine in a large dose is a poison.' This has been true since ancient times.

Medicine

DICINE
COULD
YOU OR
L YOU!
UR: YUCK)

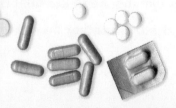

To kill germs (or bacteria) you need to use a poison that will hurt only the germs that cause illness, because most of the germs that live in and on us are very good for us.

MACHO MEDICINE

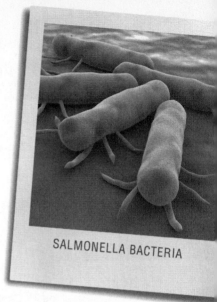

SALMONELLA BACTERIA

In a part of Austria called Styria, the men used to be . . . well, a bit macho. Perhaps they still are – this is the part of Austria that Arnold Schwarzenegger was born in. It's unlikely he would do what the men of the area used to do as a hobby, though. They used to eat arsenic!

The purpose, they said, was to improve their 'wind', so they could go faster, up and down the hills and mountains of Styria. Mostly, though, they seem to have done it for show, using a knife to carve some soft arsenic mineral out of a rock, and gobbling it down. From reports, the amount they took in one sitting was enough to kill a large horse, but it was very insoluble, and would have passed through their gut long before it was absorbed.

About the time the modern Olympic Games began, people got the idea that strychnine was good for endurance runners and cyclists. Even today, some weight-lifters take strychnine.

End of a legend

It is highly likely that the famous Australian horse, Phar Lap, was poisoned when a vet gave him a small amount of strychnine, not realising that the horse was already being doped with the same poison to make him run faster.

LUCKY LOUIS

King Louis XIV of France was the famous French
king we see being served by the Three Musketeers.
The Musketeers are invented characters, but King
Louis was real. He ruled France for more than 60 years,
starting when he was just five. At the age of 20, he
almost died, thanks to a medical treatment he was
given, antimony wine. This was prepared by leaving
vinegary wine to stand in a jug made of antimony.
The wine slowly dissolved some of the metal.
The amount of antimony absorbed by the patient
depended on the type of wine and the purity of the
antimony. This preparation was remarkably risky, and
if luck had not been running Louis' way, history could
easily have been rather different. As it was, he survived,
and his kingdom flourished.

Poisons like that made the patients feel awful, so
after they got over the poisoning, they felt much better,
and paid their doctors well. That sort of poison was
very good for the doctors.

Bad mix for monks

According to Samuel Johnson, who wrote the first real English dictionary, antimony got its name after an abbot gave pigs an antimony supplement in their feed. The pigs thrived on it. Inspired by this, the abbot fed the same mix to his monks. The monks sickened and died, causing the mix to be called *antimonachus*, meaning 'bad for monks'. Even if this is untrue, it tells us that antimony was known to be unpleasant stuff in the mid-1700s when Johnson was writing. It was mostly used in tartar emetic, a poison used to make a patient vomit up whatever else might be troubling him or her.

POLISHING OFF GERMS

Some of the best of all the medical
poisons are antibiotics,
which we have been using
to save lives since the 1940s.

The name says it all: *anti-*,
meaning against, *-biotic*, meaning life. The good news
is that antibiotics are not very poisonous to us, but they
are very poisonous to bacteria, the germs that cause so
many illnesses. Germs are not all the same, though, and
so you need to have the right antibiotic, one that will
get to the right part of your body, and it has to be an
antibiotic that kills the problem germs, because germs
can be as different as dolphins and mice!

In the last 70 years, many bacteria
have become immune to some
antibiotics, which means that
bacterial infections doctors
treated in the 1930s
have started to come
back again.

We can become immune as well. The bacteria in our stomachs make as much alcohol as one standard drink each day. Alcohol is a poison, but in small doses we can deal with it. Our bodies make a special sort of chemical, an enzyme, that breaks down the alcohol. It takes time, but that is how people get over being drunk.

Warning! Drinking this might make you drunk.

A MAGIC BULLET?

One interesting new method of medical poisoning uses clever tricks to attach poisons to things that are not wanted. The idea actually began in the early 1900s, when scientists realised that some sorts of dye attach to some types of bacteria, but it was never all that useful.

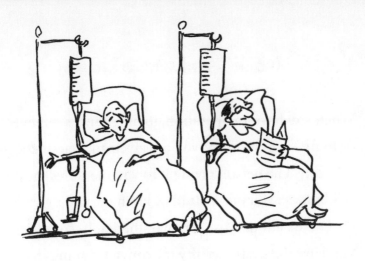

Now researchers are planning to use ricin (riss-in), a very powerful poison, attached to a chemical that is like a cancer magnet, so the ricin molecule gets dragged along until the cancer magnet finds a cancer cell. That will put a poison molecule up close to the cancer cell, and let it go, so that it can move in and kill the cancer cell.

Nobody is certain that this sort of method will work yet, but scientists hope that one day, a very small amount of poison, properly delivered, could be the best way to make cancer sufferers healthy again.

MEDICAL EXECUTIONS

When you have an operation, to have tonsils removed or to fix a major injury, you are given an anaesthetic – a poison. The person giving it to you measures the dose so it knocks you out instead of killing you.

There's another use for anaesthetics. In countries that have the death penalty for convicted murderers, a lethal injection is sometimes thought to be the kindest method of execution.[5] The process usually begins with a sedative, a calming drug that stops the prisoner feeling too much fear. The killer injection itself is an anaesthetic, and the dose is increased until it's enough to cause death.

There was once a law that allowed for a much more cruel punishment.

In 1531, a cook called Richard Coke tried to poison the bishop of Rochester.

[5] In Australia we think it's more humane not to execute criminals at all, so the question of method doesn't come up.

He missed his target and poisoned two other people instead. Even so, King Henry VIII was very, very annoyed. As far as he was concerned, poisoning or trying to poison one of his bishops was treason. Richard Coke was sentenced to be boiled to death in public. Nobody, especially kings and queens, liked murderers very much.

7

'NOT ME, YOUR HONOUR': GREAT POISONERS IN HISTORY

The funny thing about the Great Poisoners is that they were really the Great Failures, the ones who got caught. The true Great Poisoners never got caught, so we don't know who they were.

Bassawur Singh caught himself with his own poison in the end, and so did the Borgias, but other poisoners were just not as clever as they thought. The poisoner has to know what they are doing. They need the right dose, and they need to choose the right poison for the task.

DEATH BY DATURA

Bassawur Singh was a professional thief and occasional murderer in India in the 1800s. He would give people food that contained poisons, usually just enough to knock them out so he could rob them, but sometimes a bit more. Once, as he shared some of his special food, the thief ate some himself to make his victims less suspicious. When they fell unconscious, he robbed them. Once again, Bassawur Singh expected that poison would be useful to him.

This time, though, he ate too much of the food. After his victims came around and reported the theft to police, Singh was found some distance away, completely unconscious. He never revived. All the stolen property was recovered, along with a supply of the datura seeds he used to add to the food he so 'kindly' gave away.

THE BORGIA FAMILY

The Borgias were a ruling family in Italy around 500 years ago. They were rich and powerful, and two of them became Pope at different times. They were not nice people. There are many tales about Lucrezia Borgia and her brother Cesare, and how they poisoned people who got in their way. The stories are probably exaggerated, and nobody even knows what poison they used. A Scottish expert tells me he thinks it was arsenic oxide, but I think it was sugar of lead (the *sapa* the Romans used in their wine), and other people have different theories again.

Whatever it was, the Borgias did well from poisons,

because they ruled by fear. So long as people believed
that they had access to deadly poisons and knew how to
use them, the fear would continue. On the other hand,
there's a story that at least one of the Borgias died
when he drank a poisoned bottle of wine by mistake.

THE BOCARMÉS BOTCH THE JOB

If you were looking for a complete failure at poisoning,
Count Hyppolite de Bocarmé would be a top
candidate. The penniless Count set out to poison his

wife's brother with nicotine in 1849. He and his wife
killed the brother because he had money that the
Countess would inherit. They succeeded in killing him,
but then their luck ran out.

The Count had done some research about nicotine
but he wasn't very good at hiding what he was up to.
He made several mistakes, like asking people about
how to prepare nicotine, and practising on cats and
ducks, then burying the
bodies. He should have
used up-to-date
books in a
library, and
burned the dead
cats and ducks.
It was just
the Count's bad luck,
though, that his research was a bit behind
the times. He had read or been told that scientists could
not trace nicotine in a body, but by 1849, scientists
could detect nicotine in a body if the conditions were
just right. And the Count made conditions just right.

BIRDIE

Nicotine smells (if you have ever been near a smoker, you will know how horrible it is), so the Count poured vinegar down his dead brother-in-law's throat. Meanwhile his wife tried to scrub stains off the timber floor of the room where her brother had died.

Vinegar is a mild acid, and the thing scientists needed to be able to detect nicotine was for the body to be treated with a mild acid. The Count had done the one thing that would make sure he was caught. He was found guilty, and went to the guillotine to be beheaded. His wife claimed that he had made her do it, so she was let off, and presumably inherited her brother's money.

Nicotine is quite poisonous, even if you don't take it through your mouth or lungs. When tobacco pickers are working, they hold the bunch of leaves under their armpits. Nicotine soaks through their skin, making them dizzy and causing vomiting. Tobacco companies prefer not to tell smokers that what they put in their mouths has been in some farm worker's armpit!

CLEOPATRA AND HER COBRA?

Poisoning has always been 'something we don't do, but foreigners do it all the time'. The English accused the French of being poisoners, the French said it was the Italians and the Romans, the Romans said it was the Greeks and the Egyptians, the Greeks blamed the Persians, and so it went.

This means that when you hear tales about 'foreign' poisoners, you are probably hearing a yarn, a made-up story. The Romans regarded Cleopatra, Queen of Egypt, as a foreigner, and told stories of how she tested poisons on her prisoners (or on her lovers, in some versions). She is supposed to have committed suicide by allowing a snake to bite her, rather than be captured by the Romans and paraded as a prisoner in the streets of Rome.

In an odd sort of way, because the snake's venom saved her from ridicule, even that poison did some sort of good for Cleopatra.

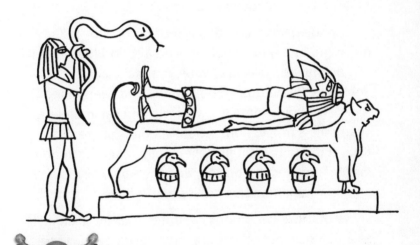

In one of his plays, William Shakespeare has Cleopatra being bitten by an asp, but if she really died of snakebite, it was much more likely to have been from a cobra.

FANGS AND STINGS: ANIMAL POISONS

Cleo's Cobra is one of many animals that use poisons, either to catch or paralyse their prey, or to defend themselves against other animals that want to eat them. Spiders, snakes and toads make their own poisons. Other animals can eat poison plants, resist the poison, and store it to make themselves dangerous to eat.

A good example of this is tetrodotoxin or TTX. It's found in a number of fish and also in blue-ringed octopuses, seastars, crabs, marine snails and molluscs, flatworms, ribbonworms and even marine algae. On land, some frogs, newts and salamanders, carry the same venom. Scientists think some other living thing (a tiny single-celled animal or a bacterium maybe?) makes the poison, and the frogs, newts and salamanders get it second-hand.

Some of these venomous creatures use the toxin just as a defence, but others like the blue-ringed octopus use it as a way of killing prey. They will also use it to 'bite' animals which handle them, so if you ever see a brightly-coloured octopus in a rock pool, leave it alone. The bite of the octopus paralyses heart and lung muscles, but if you know CPR and keep it going long enough, you can save the life of a victim.

Many poisonous animals are brightly coloured. They seems to have found that 'it pays to advertise'. Predators quickly learn that if they eat that brightly-coloured fish or butterfly or octopus, it will taste bad or hurt (or if they learn nothing, they die). This is not much use to that particular fish, butterfly or octopus, but may save its brightly-coloured relatives from being chewed.

Some animals react more to certain poisons than others. A mongoose is unaffected by a cobra's bite, but a person will die. Humans and monkeys can be killed by a funnelweb's bite, while dogs and cats only feel a bit sick. On the other hand, chocolate is *very* bad for dogs, and it can even kill them.

Mirror, mirror on the wall, who is the poisonousest of all?

Most of us are scared of snakes. Should we be? Here are some figures on snakebite deaths.

Britain About 12 people have died from snakebite since 1900.

USA About 7000 people are bitten by snakes each year, but only 12 or so die. Many of the bites are 'dry', so no venom is injected.

Bangladesh Over 7000 snakebites, and about 1700 deaths each year.

India and Pakistan Probably 20 000 deaths from snakebite each year

So how does Australia compare?

Australia Usually has one or two deaths from snakebite each year.

Why so few deaths in Australia when we have so many dangerous snakes (see opposite)? Well, Australian snakes may be lethal, but they pretty much keep to the bush and the big wide outback. Bangladesh, India and Pakistan are much more crowded – maybe it's harder for snakes and people to avoid each other – and medical treatment is difficult to get.

The 'top ten' – the world's most poisonous snakes

Inland Taipan *Oxyuranus microlepidotus*	Australia	One bite may contain enough venom to kill 100 adults
Saw-scaled Viper *Echis carinatus*	Middle East Asia	The biggest killer in Africa, with venom five times as toxic as the cobra's
Australian Brown Snake *Pseudonaja textilis*	Australia	Just 3 milligrams (half a teaspoon) of its venom can kill an adult human
Krait *Bungarus candidus*	Southeast Asia and Indonesia	Half of the bites from this snake are fatal even when treated
Taipan *Oxyuranus scutellatus*	Australia	One bite can kill up to 12 000 guinea pigs
Tiger Snake *Notechis scutatus*	Australia	Aggressive, kills more people than any other Australian snake
Hooknosed Sea Snake *Enhydrina schistosa*	Arabian Sea to Coral Sea	Very strong venom, but bites only if provoked
Coral Snake *Micrurus fulvius*	North America	Strong venom but small ones cannot deliver enough venom to kill a human
Boomslang *Dispholidus typus*	Africa	The most dangerous rear-fanged snake in the world
Death Adder *Acanthophis antarcticus*	Australia and New Guinea	Kills half its victims unless they get anti-venom

8

'SOUP, DEAR?':

POISONERS AT HOME

Some of the most famous
poison cases of the
nineteenth century
happened in people's
homes. Lawyers
say that husbands
poisoned wives and wives poisoned husbands because
no one had thought of divorce in those days. But part
of the problem was that some poisons were easy to get,
and hard to detect. Once scientists found ways to detect
the easy poisons, poisoning became less common.

THE POISON DOCTORS

Edward Pritchard was, it seems, an unpleasant fellow. He was working as a doctor in Glasgow in 1865, and by then he had been married for 15 years. He was tired of his wife, Mary, and set out to kill her with poison so he could marry the housemaid. As a doctor, of course, he could get as much poison as he needed.

When his wife became ill, her mother came to nurse her, but she was in the house for only one day before she fell ill as well, and died on 25 February. Mary died on 18 March. Pritchard had the coffin unscrewed so he could kiss the lips of the wife he had poisoned, an act which had him labelled later 'the Human Crocodile'.

An anonymous letter to the authorities made them suspect Pritchard. The women's bodies were dug up, and enough antimony was found to justify a verdict of murder. Pritchard was sent to the gallows.

There were other doctor-poisoners as well, like George Lamson. The story starts with a law expert, Professor Robert Christison, giving evidence in a court case in Scotland. Christison started to explain that there was only one substance which couldn't be traced by doctors, but the judge interrupted him before he could name it. According to the judge, it was better not to give the public this information. Back at the university, among his students, Christison named the substance as aconitine. In his audience sat a medical student named George Lamson, who later became Dr Lamson.

In March 1882, George Lamson was tried and swiftly convicted and executed for poisoning his brother-in-law, Percy Malcolm John. Percy John was a paraplegic, and Lamson was supposedly showing him how to put 'sugar' in a gelatine capsule as a way of taking nasty medicine. Lamson had bought two grains of aconitine a few days earlier, and it was this drug, said the prosecution, that was actually in the capsules.

The bad news for Lamson was that forensic science had moved forward since his student days. The poison was identified, and he swung for his crime (was hanged). A little knowledge is a dangerous thing, when you set out to kill with poison.

Can babies be poisoners?

It's hard to imagine, but in a way it's true. As a baby takes shape inside its mother, it releases small amounts of poison to kill certain cells. For example, a fetus at one stage has flippers, not hands. By killing the cells that would otherwise web the fingers together, poison makes the flipper into a hand.

THE PERFECT POISON

These days, you don't see as many murders with poison. Why? Mainly because the few poisons that have no taste and make the death seem a natural one are hard to get and easy for police to identify. There are still plenty of poisons in our homes, but each one has an unpleasant taste or a horrible smell, so that everyone is warned.

A good murder poison has to be just right.

- First, it has to be available, preferably without anybody noticing that you are getting some of it.
- Next, it needs to be tasteless and colourless, so the victim doesn't notice that he or she is being poisoned.
- Last, it has to cause symptoms that make it look just like a natural death.

Those were the main rules for getting away with murder in ancient times. These days there is one more rule.

- The poison has to be one which cannot be detected in the victim after death. In fact, by the time you have worked through the list, there are only one or two poisons that fit. I could tell you what they are, but then I would have to kill you . . .

 Nearly 200 years ago, a German man was walking down a dark passage when he noticed that the soup his wife had made him was glowing in the dark. She ended up in jail when the police found it contained phosphorus rat poison. She had made a bad choice.

PETER MACINNIS lives in Sydney and his friends refer to him as a fact-fossicker. He became interested in poisonous things when he saw a blown-up picture of a spider that looked just like his Latin teacher. (The spider was harmless, but the Latin teacher was venomous.) Later he trained as a biologist and came to realise just how much of Nature is poisonous, one way or another.

His hobbies include climbing small mountains slowly, and sitting on top of small mountains wondering how to get down again.

BETTINA GUTHRIDGE has never poisoned anyone – so far. She's been too busy illustrating over 100 books, including *Matilda and the Dragon* and *My Mum Tarzan*. Her favourite project was writing and illustrating 'Travel Solos', a series of six books about different countries. Her dream now is to travel to more exotic places and draw beautiful pictures of them.

THANKS

The publishers would like to thank istockphoto.com and the following photographers for images used in the text: page i and throughout text Linda Bucklin (skull & cross bones); pages vi and 61 Renaud Gombert (pills); page viii Linda Bucklin (gas mask, also page 53), Samantha Grandy (toast), blackred (modern pill bottle, also page 56) & Suzannah Skelton (rattlesnake, also page 76); page 1 leezsnow (sprayer); page 2 Kelly Cline (coffee); pages 3, 17, 34, 39, 41, 44, 60, 86 Clayton Hansen (aged paper background); pages 21, 23, 31, 55, 58, 81 Stefan Klein (taped paper); page 36 Vasko Miokovic (varnish); page 56 William Fawcett (antique medicine bottle) & Dane Wirtzfeld (pills); page 57 Monika Wisniewska (salmonella bacteria) & Greg Nicholas (polaroid); page 62 Liz Van Steenburgh (wine bottle/opener); page 63 Brian Eggertsen (stethoscope); page 64 Andrea Leone (syringe); page 81 Jaimie D. Travis (boy in flippers).

Warning

Want to find out more about poisons?
Then remember this.

I suppose it's not surprising that when I started asking questions about poisons, people began looking at me rather strangely. When I told visitors that the path beside my workplace often has enough of a poison (I could tell you it was ricin, but then I would have to kill you) on it to kill 3000 people, they left quite quickly. Even close friends seem nervous when I pull out my copy of *Murrell's Poisons*. Think about it before you tell your friends or teachers that you're keen to become an expert on all things toxic. (Then again, it could be a good thing to tell teachers that make a habit of tormenting students . . .)

There's one good thing, though. No one wants to share my chocolate biscuits any more.

WHERE TO FIND OUT MORE

Books for kids

Jim Morelli, *Poison! How to Handle the Poisonous Substances in Your Home*, Andrews and McMeel, Kansas City, 1997

Struan Sutherland and Susie Kennewell, *Take Care! Poisonous Australian Animals*, 3rd edition Hyland House, Melbourne, 1999

Publications for teachers

John Emsley, *The shocking history of phosphorus : a biography of the devil's element*, Macmillan, London, 2000

Peter Macinnis, *The Killer Bean of Calabar and Other Stories*, Allen & Unwin, Sydney, 2004

Mary Matossian, *Poisons of the past : molds, epidemics, and history*, Yale University Press, New Haven, 1989

Adrienne Mayor, *Greek Fire, Poison Arrows and Scorpion Bombs*, Woodstock Books, New York, 2003

Cathy Newman and Cary Wolinski, 'Pick Your Poison', *National Geographic*, May 2005

Websites

A lot of information on the Web can't be trusted, but if you use the right search words, you have more chance of getting reliable facts. Try

- heavy metals such as **lead, cadmium, thallium** or **mercury**
- plant poisons known in ancient times – **aconite, agaric, belladonna, colocynth, digitalis, hemlock, strychnine, wormwood**
- more recent poisons like **DDT, diethylene glycol, dioxins, mustard gas, organophosphates** and **PCBs**
- you could also try **alkaloid, antibiotics, toxin, venom**

And try these sites:

Victorian Poisons Information Centre: • www.rch.org.au/poisons/

Queensland Poisons Information Centre: • www.health.qld.gov.au/PoisonsInformationCentre/default.htm

A good account of poisons affecting pets: • www.leather-creations.com/newsletter/chewed_boot_3.html

A fascinating case study:
• www.pharmj.com/Editorial/20001223/articles/arsenic.html

• www.wellcome.ac.uk

INDEX